Scale Your Sales

Avoid the 7 Critical Mistakes CEOs Make

Walter Crosby

Helix Sales Development

Exclusive Reader Resources

As a special gift for readers of *Scale Your Sales: Avoid the 7 Critical Mistakes CEOs Make*, I have created an exclusive webpage where you can download resources that help you and your team correct the 7 mistakes and other challenges within the sales organization. These include:

- The framework for creating strong accountability.

- A link to a sales process grader that identifies the strengths and weaknesses of your current sales process.

- A link to a workbook for your sales leader that explains the steps required to fix your revenue forecast.

- A link to a free trial of a sales candidate assessment that I use to predict sales success.

- Samples of coaching dashboards that identify a rep's strengths and weaknesses.

- A link to help you understand how your sales organization compares to your competitors.

- An onboarding checklist to improve onboarding and give a sales rep a faster start.

- And more...

www.waltercrosby.com/resources

To my amazing wife, Heidi, who is always supportive of my unconventional journey to grow professionally, follow my passion, and provide value to my clients.

Contents

PART I

Who Should Read this Book?

I wrote this book with a particular person in mind: the visionary leader who must create a sales driven organization and grow revenue, but struggles to understand their own sales organization. My objective is to shine a light on the problems that might be in your blind spots, and help you remove the obstructions that keep getting in the way, once and for all.

This book was written for the CEO who must save time fixing the issues with the sales team. Time is our most precious resource. A leader's time has many demands, yet must be balanced with obligations from your family, friends, and, of course, your business. The walk along this balance beam of life is challenging.

The intended reader is a business owner, an entrepreneur, or a leader who is committed to reaching their big vision. They may not have adopted the moniker, but they are a Visionary Leader. My reader is committed to reaching their goals, but have concerns with the sales organization.

When I write about growing revenue, I mean significant growth—two-times growth in three to five years. This book is for that CEO. I want to help the CEO realize their vision! Is that you?

These leaders have something in common. They have grown their business to the current level by sheer will and grinding it out, following their passion. They have reached an inflection point, and just cannot put their finger on the reason the revenue forecast is always off, or they cannot get the sales team to perform at a high level, or their team keeps hiring the wrong salespeople. Perhaps the sales leader does understand the business strategy, and another issue might be that the way the salespeople talk about their product is ineffective.

The CEO is frustrated, concerned, and pissed off the sales organization is under-performing. Revenue is sometimes off 35% from budget. They have a superior product that should command a premium price, yet the sales team needs discounts to close deals.

I wrote this book for the CEO who has the desire and commitment to take the journey along the bumpy road called transformation, because at the end of the road is their freedom and their vision realized. I wrote this book for that Visionary Leader.

This book is going to communicate what high priced sales trainers don't want you to know, and the reasons sales training does not work. The 7 Critical Mistakes I describe are common in small companies and in large companies. U.S. companies spend over $70 billion annually on training. $4.6 billion is on sales training. The average spend per salesperson is $1,495. Yet, most sales training fails to deliver lasting results.

I implore you to take corrective action outlined in the following pages. Stop throwing money at a problem without gathering the data that identifies the underlying problems. There are actionable ideas in this book and questions to ask your team. Use them, please.

Who is this book not written for?

This book is NOT written for the CEO who:

- Will not accept some of the responsibility for the sales team's current condition.

- Expects the work to be easy.

- Expects the effort to be free of conflict and push-back from the sales team.

- Just wants a Band-Aid when it is clear there is a gaping wound in sales.

- Doesn't care about transformation and just wants quick fixes to move the needle for the next quarter.

I am going to share solutions to the underlying problems in the sales organization. If that sounds good to you, go grab a cocktail, maybe a cigar, and strap in for a look behind the sales development curtain.

My Promise to You

If you are still reading, I promise not to waste your valuable time. The intent is to shine a light on problems that exist in your business, and provide you actionable ideas and a path to correct the obstructions in the sales organization.

I believe CEOs make great decisions when they have good information and data. It will take about ninety minutes to read this book. In that time, I will share insights from my thirty-five years of sales experience, real data from over 2.2 million evaluations of salespeople, and battle-tested solutions to challenge your team.

I promise to do my part and explain the misconceptions about the sales organization that cause mistakes. Everyone is "in sales," especially the CEO. Although sales is not your role within your company, it is your responsibility. CEOs must define the company's sales story, ensure the direction and strategy of the sales team is aligned with their vision, and ultimately hold the sales organization to high performance standards.

This book is written in my voice, which is about delivering ideas in clear, simple language. It is sometimes blunt. It is always honest. My intent with this book, and my approach to coaching, is summed up in this quote from legendary NFL Coach, Tom Landry.

> *"A coach is someone who tells you what you <u>don't</u> want to hear, who has you see what you <u>don't</u> want to see, so you <u>can be</u> who you have always known you could be."*

I want to help you elevate your sales organization. There isn't a **magic wand**. If you want transformational results, you need work on the fundamentals that create the change.

For my part of your transformation, I will:

- Identify the common misconceptions about sales organizations and salespeople that cause poor performance.

- Provide data that will show why you should be more selective about the salespeople you hire, and illustrate that less than 50% of all salespeople are worth your development resources.

- Share a framework to create accountability, and root out mediocrity from your sales organization.

- Share a path to understanding your sales force's strengths and weaknesses—the people and the systems.

If you are serious about transforming your sales organization, I have created a resource page just for you, the reader. You have access to tools that I use to coach and grow sales leaders, managers, and reps. You will be armed with the information that you need to make better decisions, and drive sales performance through your leadership. You can find those resources at:

www.waltercrosby.com/resources

Introduction

There are four things I want you to know about me that will put some context to my approach. First, I have been trying to elevate the sales profession since I was twelve years old. Yes, twelve, but back then I didn't realize I was behaving differently. I had a paper route starting at twelve until I was seventeen. This was back when the paper was delivered to the home, and was actually paper. The routes grew larger as I grew. I was earning $40 a week as a twelve-year-old, and over $200 a week at the end.

I learned about customer service, listening to customers early, and tips. People wanted the paper delivered to a very specific spot at the house; if I did that well, I earned tips. Give the people what they want consistently! I tried to share this concept with other kids to improve everyone's performance.

The second thing you should know is I grew up in a blue-collar home. We had dinner together every night. I learned about life, hard work, and effort at the dinner table from my parents. I put myself through the University of Michigan by working and with student loans—loans that I paid back.

I was told by my high school counselor not to apply to Michigan. I was not a fit. I had the grades and scores, but culturally I would be a fish out of water. A sure way to get me to succeed is to tell me I can't or shouldn't. The takeaways from my time in Ann Arbor were how to navigate a diverse group of people with whom I had little in common, as well as finding my way through a huge institution that barely noticed the individual.

The third item is that I am passionate about helping visionary leaders of B2B businesses turn their companies into a sales-driven organization. This requires me to help the leader realize their vision when they do not have a clear picture of how to do that. Again, there is not a magic wand, or a one-size-fits-all approach. It does include working on the same fundamentals. These fundamentals are:

- **Evaluation and Improvement Analysis:** Understanding of the strengths and weaknesses of the people in the sales organization, the systems, and leadership.

- **Sales culture**: Establishing a high-performance culture and to stop accepting mediocrity.

- **Sales Structure**: Sales systems, processes, and sales roles with clarity of purpose and expectations.

- **Salespeople:** Attract and retain better salespeople.

- **Sale Management:** Elevate sales management. The sales managers struggle to know what to do. Let's give them a fighting chance.

- **Sales Leadership:** Similar to sales managers, they need structure and a framework to support your vision.

I don't have an MBA. I don't have a history working at large corporations or institutions. The companies I worked at were run by entrepreneurs who had a passion for their business. I often competed for business against huge international organizations. I learned from mentors, entrepreneurs, competitors, customers, and books.

I am a roll-up-my-sleeves, get-it-done sales guy who speaks passionately and bluntly about sales. I advocate for salespeople and sales managers who demonstrate a desire to learn and upskill. Most importantly, I share the vision of the CEO entrepreneur who is at the helm, and needs collaboration to create a sales organization that scales.

The fourth thing about me is that I am a lifelong learner. I am constantly learning from clients and sharpening my skills. I model the behaviors I teach sales managers and salespeople. I have aligned myself with best-in-class sales development partners: Objective Management Group and Membrain. The goal is to give my clients an edge against their competition, and take market share from their competitors.

My clients' dreams become mine. I operate like my income is dependent upon my clients' success. If we cannot grow revenue and improve the sales organization more than 40%, let's not start. My work is about lasting results for clients.

The mistakes described in this book are from repeated real-life situations I have witnessed and experienced. The solutions are battle-tested and work. They are not easy, but effective.

PART II

Chapter 1

Critical Mistake #1

Not aligning your vision with an individual's authority.

The mistake CEOs make with sales culture is the same mistake made with company culture. The words from leadership are not connected to the actions and behaviors the team must execute each day. Each employee has authority at their level of function. The behaviors, activities, and attitude they control in their role—their job. They are afraid to make mistakes or to change. I will explain with an example.

Brenda, the president of a growing security integrator, wanted to improve the company culture. She worked with the leadership team at their off-site meeting to gain clarity on her vision for the company. Brenda and the team wanted the company to be viewed as best in class by their customers.

After the off-site, their "north star" was crystal clear—<u>elevate the customer experience</u>. The focus was the customer.

Their "north star" was rolled out at a company-wide meeting, and the VPs of each division spoke to their teams about the objectives. All 145 employees were excited, and the feedback back to Brenda was positive. The organization was on board with her vision. A customer survey was completed to give the team a benchmark.

Fast forward six months, and the results from a second customer survey results came back. There was no change in the results. The team had not elevated the customer experience. The results in nine and twelve months showed a small reduction in satisfaction.

Why would an objective that the entire organization found motivating fail?

The answer is simple. Brenda did not connect the dots for the employees. Brenda and the leadership team did not help the individual employees understand what behaviors and activities they needed to change in their role at the company. In other words, a leader must give the individuals permission to do a little more, and define what the change is. Leadership did not show what the employees could do to help a customer.

The employees could not connect the dots from the concept of "a better customer experience" to what they did every day. Leadership assumed the employees would elevate. They assumed the team would figure it out. <u>The critical mistake CEOs make is not helping the employees understand what they can do within their role at the company to achieve the goal</u>.

At the 30,000-foot level, the "north star" was clear. ***Let's provide our customers with the best-in-class experience before and after the sale***. Leadership did a great job of presenting the direction the company was headed and getting the buy in from the team, yet the initiative failed.

This happens at the company level when flowery and vague language is used to speak about the big objective. It happens with the sales team as well. The direction must be clear, but the leader cannot <u>assume</u> that sales leadership and the sales team will know what they must change with their attitudes, behaviors, and activities. You have to tell them. It does not matter that they should know. What matters is that your vision and strategy is executed well.

The changes can, and should be, collaborative. However, even the most motivated employees will get back to the daily grind of their role and fall back into habits that served them in the past. Nothing will change. Give the team the support they need to change what they do each day in their role that move the needle. Don't assume they will figure it out.

How do you fix this mistake with the sales organization?

The sales leader in the organization must set and manage clear expectations for the salespeople to transform the sales culture. The expectations must help the company achieve its goals. And this is critical—the expectations must be connected to the salespeople's personal goals. The rep must see how making the calls and having meetings with decision makers will generate the commissions that the rep needs to achieve their personal goals. The boat they want. The bigger house they need. The college education fund that must grow.

The sales leader and the sales manager need to carry this message to the team every day, every week, and every month. What does the rep need to change to achieve the goal? The expectations cannot be vague.

What are the steps required to create a high-performance sales culture?

1. **Clear Vision:** Your vision in the context of how you want the brand to be perceived internally and externally.

2. **Connect the Dots**: Define the attitudes, behaviors, and activities the sales reps must achieve daily, weekly, and monthly to achieve the company objectives and their personal goals.

3. **Manage the Process**: Clear expectations will require accountability, repeated communication of your vision, and coaching of the team for improvement. This is key is to <u>never accept mediocrity</u>.

Let's dive in.

Clear vision is often the easiest for an entrepreneur to define. You know your purpose. You have passion, otherwise you would not have made the personal sacrifices it takes to build a company. Being a visionary leader, you articulate who you want to help and why. It must go beyond an eight-figure exit. The vision must connect with your team and your customers.

Start with your leadership team to crystalize the fine points, and consider how you roll this out with vigor and passion to the company. Use simple language with clear objectives that the entire organization can get behind. What are your core values, your vision for three, five, and ten years? What are the steps to achieve your vision in the next twelve months and quarter by quarter.

Once you have your vision, you can collaborate with the leadership team to deliver this into the sales organization. You will need to confirm and test the sales leader on messaging the ideas to the team. Do they and the sales managers know the personal goals of the reps and how to connect the personal goals to your vision? All of this fails if they don't! Salespeople can be cynical. Make sure the sales leader and sales manager can tie your vision to motivation for the salespeople!

Connecting the dots can be the fun part because this is where the growth happens for the team. Don't rely exclusively on the sales leader to carry the message. You are the best storyteller in the company. It is your vision, and the salespeople need you to help them put it into context for the customers and prospects. The reps don't have your business acumen—help them understand what best in class means! They don't know. From time to time, show up to a sales meeting and sell the vision!

The sales managers and sales leaders set the expectations for the team. Collaborate with the sales leader. The expectations must cover three buckets.

1. **GRIT:** You want salespeople who have the commitment and desire to close business. I call this "Will to Sell." Commitment, Desire, Outlook, Motivation, and Responsibility. Non-negotiable.

2. **Behaviors:** The salespeople must conduct themselves as professionals. They must follow the sales process, follow sales methodology, participate in sales meetings, be open to coaching, and be competitive but willing help other team members. The reps' interactions with your customers and prospects must be congruent with your brand and your vision.

3. **Activities:** High-performance sales teams have sales managers and sales leaders who clearly define the standards. Excellence looks like "this."

Weak performance looks like "this." *We don't tolerate mediocrity* is the message in the interview, the monthly sales strategic meeting, and one-on-one meetings. The intolerance is tempered with coaching, skill development, and support for the salespeople who are struggling. There must be clear metrics for high-performance that are measured weekly and monthly.

The salespeople, just like any other employee, must know the standards that are expected in their role every day. The salespeople must be clear on who your ideal client is and what that ideal client's pain points are. That is the minimum. They need to know how their attitudes, behaviors, and activities are connected to your vision. You will need to tell the story a lot. Rinse and repeat consistently.

Your sales managers don't manage the salespeople. That's right, trying to manage salespeople is chaos. The sales manager must manage the process, the metrics, the pipeline, and the expectations. *More on this later.* Accountability is not a bad word. Accountability to standards are what elite salespeople strive to exceed. If you have an accountability problem, you have the wrong people in the sales seat or the sales management seat. Elite salespeople expect accountability and coaching. Get more elite salespeople.

Questions for contemplation.

- Have you shared your vision with the sales team consistently and clearly enough for them to understand why it is important?

- Does each member of the team understand what they can do and should do to create more wins?

- Are there clear expectations for what the salespeople need to do every day and every week to achieve your vision?

- Do the sales leaders manage the process creating strong accountability?

- Are the right people in the right seats?

Chapter 2

Critical Mistake #2

Allowing salespeople to tell a story instead of your story.

Do your proposals devote significant page space explaining the company history, milestones of the company's growth, or a list of accomplishments?

Can the salespeople articulate three to five things that make them different from your competition? The reps must be able to talk about it in the context of solving problems that buyers care about.

Go ask the salespeople this question:

If a prospect asks, "Why are you different from [name a competitor]," what do you say?

WALTER CROSBY

The answers might surprise you. One or two of the salespeople may be able to give you three differentiators that identify the outcomes your company creates. The others might list features of the products/services that they think are important.

<u>The critical mistake CEOs make is allowing the company sales story to be ineffective</u>. The sales leader should have the skills to collaborate, but the responsibility to ensuring it is effective and congruent falls to the CEO (like so many other aspects of the business).

Another big problem is that the answers will vary from rep to rep, and they will not be about outcomes that prospects and customers care about. That inconsistency and lack of focus on the buyer's needs is the problem.

Do you think inconsistent messaging could be a cause for inconsistent results? The salespeople should not sound like robots. However, everyone should be on the same page. The messaging should be like sheet music for a musician. Everyone is playing in the same key and at the same tempo. The salespeople should be able to play the sheet music in their own style, but play all of the notes!

28

Consider a few great jazz trumpeters for a moment.

- Louis Armstrong.

- Dizzy Gillespie

- Miles Davis

- Chet Baker

- Wynton Marsalis

- Freddie Hubbard

Each sound different. In fact, any one of these great trumpeters could play about three notes of the same song and a jazz fan could identify who was playing.

I bring this up early because it is important to know that salespeople must be authentic to their style and personality. Their style and delivery represents the art of sales. However, the science of sales is having the right combination of words—the sheet music—and messaging that positions the products in the mind of the buyer as a solution to their problems!

Buyers make decisions based on their criteria, but they all boil down into three reasons the prospect buys. Your messaging will likely not be compelling if it doesn't address at least one of these three categories.

1. **Time:** The message needs to be in the context of saving time.

2. **Money:** The message must show how the product makes the buyer money or saves them money.

3. **Risk:** The messaging should illustrate how the offering mitigates the buyer's risk to a problem they have.

How do you know if the message is on point? The buyers. Here is the litmus test for the messaging. ***So what?*** If a buyer responds *so what*, the words did not resonate. Further refinement or a great follow-up question is necessary to get the buyer to see the solution to the problem they did not know existed.

Let's discuss an assumption so many entrepreneurs make. The typical CEO assumes that the sales leader will create the appropriate messaging or worse, assume the salespeople know how to do this. Neither do! Objective Management Group has data on 2.25M salespeople. The data is clear.

- 6% of salespeople are elite

- 20% are good

- 74% are average, weak, and ineffective

The sales team needs help telling a compelling sales story. They also need help identifying the decision makers at the ideal companies. I call them strategic targets. They need a list of companies, and a description of who that buyer is. A persona of the decision maker.

Frankly, and this will sting a little, it is the business leader's responsibility to create the strategic targets and the positioning of the products in the buyer's mind. The leader may need to seek help and collaboration—but who is better at telling the company story than the Visionary Leader?

Positioning the company's offerings does not need to be overly complicated. In the remainder of this chapter, I will share a formula and the frameworks we use in a workshop to fix this critical mistake.

The framework is simple. Not all aspects of this framework are used at the same time, but everything the sales team will need to execute—including outbound calls, outbound emails, social media messaging, and to differentiate effectively—is identified in the framework.

First, the broad framework. I will help define the framework and, finally, provide my example so you can see a working model. Some of the ideas can stand on their own, and others work together.

1. **Who am I**? A very concise and to the point description of what you do, how you help, and for whom.

   I am a sales consultant and sales coach. I only work with dedicated CEOs at mid-market companies who are committed to realizing the vision by increasing revenue and boosting profit.

2. **Set Up Phrase**. Who do you help? This is not redundant because the context is slightly different.

   I help <u>visionary leaders</u> who...
   <u>CEOs</u> invite me in when they....

3. **Positioning the Problem**. Use emotional words to identify three to seven prospect problems the company solves in the context of time, money, and risk.

...are concerned about the time-wasted buyer's pain #1

...are frustrated with huge buyer's problem #2

...are at a loss to solving buyer's problem #3

...are facing threats from big issue #4

...are striving to achieve result #5

...are under significant pressure to eliminate buyer's pain #6

...are tired of dealing with buyer's problem #7, and need help solving it.

4. **Offerings**. Simply state what you sell. Not a pitch nor an over-embellishment.

We provide sales development and coaching programs that are easy to understand and move the needle.

We provide integrated security systems. The latest

technology, monitoring, access control, and integrated video.

We provide a digital platform accessible by a smart-phone that increases consumer participation in product contests and sweepstakes.

5. **Differentiators**. Using a transitional phrase, describe the outcomes that are different for a prospect when they use the company's products.

XYZ company continues to grow, ABC company dominates our space... because we are very different from the marketplace... because our approach is opposite of the alternatives...

We design integrated solutions with one app.

We offer in-house financing options which help clients manage capital budgets and cash flow.

Our warranty is the longest and most comprehensive in the market.

We roll up our sleeves and get in the field with your team, modeling the behaviors we coach.

This framework is collaborative. In our workshops we will have the entire sales organization, the top marketing person, and the CEO in the room. I like to start with the hardest part which is the differentiators. This requires the most significant of time. There are a lot of "so what" questions being asked to drill down to the outcomes that make a difference in your buyer's mind. This effort and time always yields better results!

Next, we move on to positioning the problem. This requires looking at the buyer's challenges from their perspective, and using the words they would use in the context of the problems they encounter every day. There are real emotions tied to these pains. The salespeople need help with the words that position their solutions to the buyer so they buy!

As an example of what this looks and sounds like when complete, I offer my messaging for Helix Sales Development. You can see how this flows together.

I am a sales consultant and sales coach. I only work with dedicated CEOs at mid-market companies who are committed to realizing their grand vision by increasing revenue and boosting profit.

CEOs invite me in when:

- The revenue forecast is inaccurate and unreliable.

- The annual turnover rate on the sales team exceeds 20%, or they are unable to retain and attract top sales talent.

- The company offers a superior product in the marketplace, but the sales team discounts to close business.

- The sales team is under-performing and leadership cannot figure out the root cause.

- The sales numbers are not meeting expectations, trending downward, and the company must add to their market share to remain viable.

I provide salespeople and sales managers coaching, sales force consulting to executives, and build consistent revenue growth with margin integrity. I am typically hired by companies committed to serious revenue growth for an exit, or to scale and realize the leader's vision.

Clients experience more success than they expect as my approach is unlike their previous attempts at sales development because:

1. My approach is simple, and I speak in honest, plain language.

2. I start with an analysis of the sales force to understand its strengths and weakness. You are given data and an ROI before I propose a solution. No canned training here.

3. I roll up my sleeves and work with your team modeling the ideas we can implement immediately while I fix the fundamental problems hidden within the sales organization that frustrate you.

4. Don't call me if you want marginal improvement. You only want to work with me if you are serious about moving the revenue needle.

5. You will be given the truth about your sales team. I am an advocate for salespeople who are fighting to get better, but once I am convinced a sales rep or sales manager is not going to succeed, I will not babysit them, or allow you to pay me to coach them.

6. I am not a recruiter. We teach your team a repeatable sales <u>specific</u> hiring process that saves you time, money, and predicts the success of candidates.

7. I am following my passion to elevate accountability within sales teams, and root out mediocrity. My engagements are personal to me, and your success is my primary driver.

It should be clear this entire story is not read aloud at once, nor is it all written out in an email. It is the backbone of all messaging. I am speaking to the individuals who I target for my services about their problems in the language they use to describe the outcomes they must have. Elements of this story can be used in conversations at a networking event, on an outbound phone call, in sales collateral, or sections can be written into emails.

Questions for contemplation.

- Is the ideal client profile and the strategic targets clear to your sales organization?

- Do they have a written down list of strategic targets that are a great fit?

- What are the pain points of the current top twenty customers that are solved by your solution?

- Can your sales team differentiate the advantages to working with your company?

- Are the salespeople still pitching features and benefits?

Chapter 3

Critical Mistake #3

Abdicating control of the sale to the buyer.

Everyone uses a calendar and understands why tracking time is important. Think of the calendar as a process—a process we all follow to navigate the year. There are events during the year that identify milestones of the journey. For example, the start of a new month, the beginning and end of the seasons, and there are holidays, birthdays, and anniversaries, too. Spring, Memorial Day, Summer, Independence Day, Autumn. Each event is a milestone to help us understand where we are in the process.

Without a calendar, humans can use the stars and the moon to identify the passage of time. It is complicated, not as accurate as a calendar, and a pain in the ass to get to an appointment on time. A calendar on your phone or the wall allows you to be precise about where you are in the moment, and the calendar allows you to easily anticipate what happens next. The calendar is a process to navigate time efficiently and effectively.

For consistent sales results, salespeople need the equivalent of a calendar. There must be a sales process and method for the buyer's journey through your company. This creates consistency in the buyer's experience regardless of the salesperson.

The sales process will support the rep in understanding where they are in the buyer's journey and what the rep must do next. The process supports sales management in accountability, performance measurement, and coaching. The sales process becomes the language in how the sales team talks about the opportunities in the sales pipeline. As you will learn in Chapter 4, the process is the conduit for an accurate revenue forecast. It is important.

A sales process represents how a salesperson navigates the buyer's journey at your company.

Similar to the months of a calendar, a sales process has stages. However, rarely are more than three to five stages required. Each stage has milestones. Milestones are what make your sales process structured and predictive of success. Accounting, operations, manufacturing, and shipping have processes and milestones to work smoothly. Frankly, it is irresponsible to not give your sales process thoughtful and professional attention. It is responsible for revenue and profit.

At Helix, I use staged, milestone centric sales process as the basis for a sales process with clients. It is called Baseline Selling©—think rounding the bases on baseball diamond. There are many sales processes available that can be effective when followed. Baseline Selling© has a huge advantage in my experience. It is a sales process for the sales team to follow, and it is a methodology.

A sales methodology is a set of principles that guides the sales reps to close opportunities. A methodology turns the goals of a stage in the sales process or series of stages into actionable steps to complete during each stage of the process. More simply, a methodology is the approach to executing the process and to qualify a prospect. It also guides the timing of questions through the stages.

Sales is not a nebulous art form that can be molded to the whims of each sales rep. Salespeople need structure. Sales is more like a high-performance car. The science is under the hood and in the frame. The art is within the design or style of the car. The science of sales resides in the sales process and methodology. The art flows from the style and personality of the salesperson to have an empathic, friendly, and buyer-focused conversation.

<u>The critical mistake that CEOs make is leaving the process that drives revenue and margin to chance</u>. What other department in the organization with critical outcomes is allowed to **wing it**? Finance? Accounts Receivable? Engineering? Manufacturing? Each has a set of standards and principles that guide the team to better outcomes and greater accuracy. Arguably the life blood of an organization, revenue creation is left to chance, or little attention is given to how the salespeople operate.

Why is revenue left to chance? There are a variety of reasons, but I believe many leaders don't understand what to do, and they assume the sales leaders have this figured out. The CEO who does not have a background in sales may have a perspective that sales is this mysterious black bag of magic that does not have a consistent structure. Even the leaders who were great salespeople in the past still do not understand how to build the structure into a sales organization. Often, they were successful salespeople despite the lack of a documented process.

Another reason, sadly, is that sales development and training companies are full of confusing approaches. There are many opinions about how and what to do, but given the general lack of trust with "salespeople," CEOs struggle to seek professional support to build out a reliable and effective toolbox for the sales organization.

The most frequent reason for not getting involved I hear from CEOs is some version of, "Isn't that the responsibility of the sales leader?" This is a logical argument, but fraught with assumptions. During the interview process of hiring the sales leader, the sales managers, or even the salespeople, does anyone inquire about what the candidates' ideas, theories, or experiences are with building sales or using a process? This critical and strategic skill set of a sales leader is not something to be left to chance.

Let's be clear, building out a sales process is not a simple exercise, nor is it impossible. The balance of the chapter is to support the Do-It-Yourself readers. It will help to follow the practical steps that are required to gain the transformation you and your team need.

Gain insights from your current team. Take the time to speak to the top producers on your sales team. Pick their brains, but be clear about what you are trying to learn. However, you must be clear <u>what</u> the salesperson is "top" at producing. What their business card says does not matter. Are they producing revenue because they are bringing new logos to the company, or are they growing current accounts? This is an important distinction. These are typically two different roles on a team. Business Development vs. Account Management.

New business development producers are Hunters in the truest sense. They have the will to prospect. They will prospect consistently. Hunters maintain a full pipeline because they know some deals will NOT close. They are also good at reaching into the strategic target accounts and talking with the decision makers.

Account managers are great at building strong relationships and handling organizational politics. They will not alienate people within the target accounts. Great account managers will manage time effectively, meet with decision-makers regularly, and <u>will</u> follow up often.

You will need to separate hyperbole from the practical steps that they follow when closing deals. Look for patterns. Interview them about two or three typical opportunities that they won, and one or two large opportunities where the wins were two to three times the average deal size. Why did they win? What did they learn in the process to get the win? Even the top sales reps will struggle with identifying how they navigate a discovery call or qualify a prospect. However, you have evidence that what the top producers are doing works. Some of the answers are between their ears!

Use the resource page to consider Baseline Selling©. It is a simple sales process that you should be able to implement with minor changes to language. It is a great guide to use for interviews with the top producers. They may use different terms and language, but most of the foundational structure of what the producers are doing is within Baseline Selling©.

In Chapter 1 we talked about accountability. The sales process is where performance is tracked. Key KPIs or sales metrics stem from a staged, milestone centric sales process:

- Win rates

- Number of new opportunities added to the pipeline

- Average time in pipeline—sales cycle

- Average opportunity size.

These four performance indicators when monitored, managed, and coached will drive revenue. They all require a sales process.

Transformation will be hard. Making changes within a sales department is no different, and perhaps worse. Expect resistance from the team. The sales leaders and or sales managers must be on board, trained, and have your support to implement. Your support means a strong commitment and desire to ride the bumpy road to more consistent revenue.

Questions for contemplation.

- Who are the top producers in the sales organization? Top at what?

- Do I have the right mix of sales roles building into my sales organization to support the areas of growth? Account Managers, New Business Development, Service Sales, Technical Sales, etc.

- Does my sales leader have the skills and business acumen that you can trust to support sales process development?

- What pieces of the puzzle am I missing? *Chapter 5 might help*.

Chapter 4

Critical Mistake #4

Accepting revenue forecasts that suck.

Does this sound familiar? The sales forecast for the next quarter hits your inbox, and you are wondering if you should discount the forecast by 25% or 35% before you take it to you take it to the advisory board. You discount the revenue because sales leadership has missed on hitting the revenue that was forecasted for six consecutive quarters.

At least once a quarter there is a bounce in revenue, but, when you look under the hood, those were the months that your margins dipped significantly. In an attempt to meet the forecast, sales leadership has authorized—even encouraged—the sales team to discount pricing to close enough deals to meet the forecasted revenue.

Your company is consistently recognized as a market leader in quality, the product team is innovative, and the marketing spend is generating marketing leads. The new sales leader requested, and you granted her, resources to upskill the salespeople in consultative selling. Nine months passed. Again, you ask yourself, why is the revenue forecast off by more than 35%?

Put a different way, as CEO, you would never accept a financial report that wasn't 100% accurate, nor would you accept a production run with a 20% failure rate. The critical mistake that CEOs make is **accepting** the revenue forecasts that are consistently wrong. It is difficult to do planning for the business when there isn't confidence in the revenue projections.

In this chapter, I am going to share what high-priced sales consultants don't want you to know. You will get the reasons why the revenue forecast is wrong, and what your sales leadership needs to do to fix it!

What is the origin of the revenue forecast?

The data for the forecast originates with opportunities in the sales pipeline. Each salesperson creates new opportunities to move through the sales process. The reps should have a metric to maintain a specific pipeline dollar value or quantity of opportunities. The value of the opportunities in the pipeline is ultimately what drives the revenue forecast. This is the moment that your revenue forecast begins to go sideways.

The revenue forecast represents the data in the sales pipeline. The data may be weighted by stage or probability of closing, but the accuracy of the projection is affected by the likelihood an opportunity will be won. So, the question to ask the sales leader is, "What is the criteria used to put an opportunity into the pipeline?" The sales leader should have clear and concise criteria. In fact, each sales rep should be able to show you how the criteria are enforced.

Think of the sales pipeline as a hallowed ground and there is a gate in front of it. The gate requires a code to enter. The metaphoric gate for the sales pipeline is the criteria. We call it a scorecard. The scorecard allows a salesperson to objectively evaluate the qualification criteria of a prospect. The scorecard must reach a certain value for the opportunity to earn the right to enter the hallowed ground of the sales pipeline.

If weak or unqualified deals are not allowed into the pipeline, several sales performance metrics are affected. For example, the sales cycle will shorten and win rates will increase because the deals have met a standard that increases the probability of closing. However, salespeople tend to feel pressure to add deals to their pipeline. They also have something we call "happy ears," which is a representation of internal optimism. The prospect said something positive that is accepted by the sales rep as a sign the deal is moving in a positive direction. Salespeople traditionally lack an appropriate amount of skepticism.

Fix this one element of the sales pipeline and you will dramatically improve the accuracy and reliability of your revenue forecast. The correction is simple in concept, but requires diligence from sales leadership and managers. The scorecard criteria must be designed based on why deals are won. What are the common characteristics of the opportunities that the team wins? Here is a list of considerations to build a scorecard to enter the sales pipeline:

- **What:** Does the prospect have a problem the company can solve?

- **Why:** Has the prospect indicated that a solution to their problem is a priority?

- **Who:** Is the rep speaking with authority or first-hand knowledge of the problem?

Sales pipeline hygiene is the responsibility of the sales leader and sales manager. They will need to be held accountable to a new standard if you are committed to fixing the revenue forecast. To help you with this task, I have included a sales leader workbook in the resource page for this book. The workbook outlines how to hold the sales leaders accountable or to assign this accountability to a suitable team member, i.e. CFO. You can find that at this link:

www.waltercrosby.com/resources

The concept of the scorecard or gate should be applied to another part of the sales process or pipeline. There should be a standard before a prospect receives a proposal. The typical proposal has information that should not land in the hands of your competitor. Things like pricing, terms, and product details are proprietary, and disseminating this information capriciously is an awful practice.

Create a criteria-based scorecard to evaluate if the salesperson has done a great job of discovery, which means the rep found a significant problem, the compelling reasons the buyer will move forward, and developed urgency to move the opportunity to a win. Yes, all three are needed in a complex B2B sale. There are common factors that increase the likelihood of a proposal addressing the prospects needs and converting to a win.

Here is a list of considerations to build a scorecard for proposal:

- Is the decision maker engaged?

- Has the problem been monetized or quantified?

- Are the criteria for a decision, and the timeline for a decision, understood?

The objective is not to make the sales pipeline smaller. It is to improve the quality of the pipeline which will have immediate impact on the accuracy of the revenue forecast.

The sales team will push back on the scorecards because it will feel like they will have to work harder. The opposite is true. They will stop being busy chasing deals that will never close.

The best practice of scorecards will challenge the concept held by many sales organizations. The idea being *anyone who raises their hand for information, opens an email, or clicks a link is a qualified prospect.* This is NOT correct. Raising the bar of entry to the pipeline will eliminate all the chasing of prospects who will never move forward and frees up the reps from working on deals that make them feel busy. They will have more time to prospect.

The scorecard criteria will need collaboration and iteration. It will impact your revenue forecast almost immediately. If you want the forecast to improve, this work is critical.

Questions for contemplation.

- Do we know why we win deals?

- Do we track how and why a deal moves through our pipeline?

- Is our pipeline value weighted objectively?

- Do we have scorecards that set salespeople up for success?

Chapter 5

Critical Mistake #5

Hiring salespeople the same way you hire everyone else.

Are all of the salespeople on the team performing? Performing means they have met or exceeded the sales objective assigned to them the last four quarters.

When I ask this question of a CEO or sales leader, the answer "yes" is less than a third of the time: ***How many of the current reps would you hire again knowing what you know about them?*** That means seven out of ten existing salespeople would not be rehired!

Again, I am referring to performance, ability to do what it takes to create wins, being a team player, and consistent effort. The individual may be a wonderful person, but look at them through the lens of their role as a salesperson.

Most entrepreneurs agree that attracting and selecting sales talent is difficult. <u>The critical mistake CEOs make is hiring salespeople the same way they hire everyone else</u>. Salespeople are different from engineers, administrative staff, or anyone else in the company. Salespeople, even the ones that are awful, are better at selling themselves than hiring managers are at objectively evaluating sales talent.

Salespeople can build rapport quickly, are comfortable meeting new people, and great at talking about themselves. If the sales hiring process is not structured, with specific information gathered from defined questions during the interview process, the average salesperson can sway the process to their advantage without anyone realizing.

The influence is compounded by pressure to hire fast and fill the empty territory, and the unconscious bias from the hiring managers. Many books have been written and research conducted on hiring biases. Some of the bias in hiring occurs overtly, but much of it happens subconsciously or without intent.

There are laws and Equal Employment Opportunity Commission (EEOC) guidelines that are in place to make sure employers do not discriminate against any protected minorities. Sales hiring should be fair, inclusive, objective, and effective at predicting success. CEOs are ultimately responsible for the hiring policies and practices of the company.

For the purposes of this chapter, I will focus on eliminating two types of bias that cause sales hiring to be ineffective:

1. Biases in favor of certain candidates.

2. Biases against certain candidates.

I will also offer solutions that can improve success and the ROI of sales candidates who are hired.

First, biases in favor of a candidate occur when a hiring manager falls in love with the experiences listed on a resume. This may include employment at a particular company held in high regard. The hiring manager can fall in love with the candidate because they are particularly charismatic, said all the right things, and the hiring manager's "gut" is saying YES! This bias and these feelings lead to so many hiring mistakes.

Second, biases against candidates fall in a parallel grouping. The candidate might have attended a university or college that does not match up with a certain pedigree, or the candidate may have had great sales experience, but the experience was outside of their industry. I knew an HR manager who outright refused to interview any candidates from an outstanding university only because she was not accepted to that institution herself. Any resume that came across her desk was dismissed because of the capricious decision.

However, the hiring mistake sounds like this—*if the candidate does not have experience in our industry, we don't want to speak with them.* This bias will eliminate candidates who may be great salespeople, who can learn quickly the specific pain points of customers, and how the company differentiates itself. This type of bias is common and costly.

The misguided belief that industry experience is always required eliminates quality salespeople. If the company's product or service is highly technical, it will take some time to gain a complete understanding of the product. The solution is to provide the salesperson a resource—the smart gal back in the office who is the product expert can be brought into opportunities that are qualified. This supports the rep getting into the field more quickly.

The real problem is a failing, retread rep hired from the industry because she had the "right experience". This rep proceeds to pitch, do demos, and write proposals to buyers who are not qualified. In other words, buyers who cannot buy or who will never buy. Good salespeople don't pitch and chase! They relentlessly prospect and qualify.

A different philosophy is to hire talent and onboard them well. If a sales candidate has good or great sales skills, the right GRIT, and a strong mindset, the sales leader can define three things for the candidate that will ensure a fast start. If the sales leader has a good onboarding plan in place for salespeople, the following can be delivered in a few days:

1. Explain to the new hire who the ideal client profile is for the product or service they will be selling, and provide the salesperson a list of at least ten strategic target companies. This should include various titles, responsibilities of the buyer, and the target company demographics.

2. Put in plain words, define the problems the buyer at the target company has, and differentiate how your company's offering solves the problems (the company sales story). Explain what frustrates and concerns the buyer.

3. Describe the three to five ways the company differentiates itself in the market.

These three points are enough for a quality salesperson to start prospecting. Of course, they will continue to gain product knowledge, market understanding, etc., but they can get to work.

To help a new sales hire succeed it will take more planning and better onboarding. In the resource page for this book there are several tools to help create a comprehensive onboarding process. Don't forget to set the expectations for the new salesperson. How will they be measured during the first week, month, quarter, and year? The new hire needs to know what accountability looks like at the company.

Of course, the new hire will need product knowledge. The new rep will become a subject matter expert eventually. The mistake made in most onboarding processes is believing the salesperson needs to know everything about the product BEFORE they hit the streets. What they need to know is who the buyer is, what problems the buyer has, and why buyers purchase from the company. Who. What. Why. Get the sales leader to focus on these issues and salespeople who have the right skills will get traction faster.

How does one improve their chances of hiring talent? I recommend a sales specific hiring process. The process I teach saves time, money, and predicts the success of sales candidates. The process is customized to company specific needs with questions and criteria. The underlying objective is to treat the sales candidates professionally and with dignity. However, I want to understand how the candidate reacts to pressure. The type of pressure they might encounter from a prospect or customer. So, the sales hiring process should ask tough questions and keep the salesperson on their heels.

The candidate is very familiar with their own career, their approach to sales, and how they think about sales, so they should be able to answer questions about themselves without struggling, deflecting, or becoming defensive. The questions that are asked through the interview process are objective and relevant to the role, and should challenge the candidate. The answers are compared and scored against defined answers that identify a weak, good, or great answer.

The cornerstone of the successful sales hiring process I teach is a **sales specific, predictive assessment**. The question that should be asked when using an assessment is, *"What do* *you want to measure?"* Go ahead think about that. What do you want to learn as a salesperson?

With salespeople, we want to understand how they think about sales and their sales skills. How an individual behaves in social settings is not predictive of whether they will sell in your markets to your customers at your price points against your competition. A colleague, Aaron Prickel, explains it this way: "You wouldn't give your son a pregnancy test to determine if he's doing drugs!"

A sales specific hiring process that includes a sales predictive assessment is a game changer for hiring better sales talent, eliminating bias, and predicting success.

"92% of salespeople recommended will rise to the top half of the sales team within twelve months."
—Objective Management Group

This is stat predictability defined because it is based on over 2.2 million evaluations and assessments in twenty-eight years. See the resource page for examples and a free trial.

www.waltercrosby.com/resources

Here are a couple more statistics from Objective Management Group:

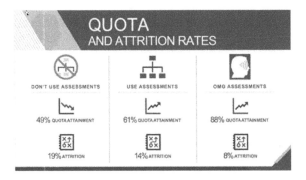

To summarize, being aware of and eliminating bias in the sales hiring process will help reduce mistakes. Improving the onboarding process for a new hire by including more information about who the customers are, why they do business with the company, and what makes the company different creates traction for a new rep. Using a sales specific hiring process with an assessment that predicts success is a game changer.

Questions for contemplation.

- Do we have a sales specific hiring process?

- What do hiring managers do to reduce or eliminate bias in recruitment?

- What can be done to strengthen the onboarding process for salespeople?

- Can our sales hiring retention and success rate improve?

Chapter 6

Critical Mistake #6

Assuming your business strategy and the sales team are aligned.

Whether the topic is a military engagement, a construction project, or growing a business, alignment between the leadership and those executing the strategies is critical for success. Operation Overlord, or D-Day, was a coordinated effort by General Dwight D. Eisenhower that involved twelve nations. It required strategic alignment for success. Weeks of planning, discussion, planning, and soul-searching was required by great military strategists to yield a victory for Allied forces.

Building a home or a large commercial structure requires alignment of design, engineering, equipment, and people in the just the right order to safely complete a well-constructed project on budget. There is a clear process, and there are standards set for each aspect of the construction process, from testing the soil to final inspections. The strategy ensures standards are set and the builders are aligned on size, materials, and timelines.

<u>The critical mistake CEOs make with strategy is NOT establishing alignment with the sales leadership team</u>. It does not matter if the sales organization is two people or 200 people, the odds of the strategies being communicated well and executed effectively is much greater with alignment.

Alignment of business strategies, marketing strategies, and sales strategies are essential. When sales leadership does not understand or agree with how the plan is to be executed, this can cause conflict within the organization and weak execution. There are many reasons for weak alignment; I will provide three examples that will provide insights to dig deeper into your sales organization.

I cannot pretend to know which specific strategies are appropriate for your business. However, I can recommend that, regardless of how you proceed, there is no time like the present to sort out differences and misalignments between your business, marketing, and sales strategies.

The three examples of potential problems with strategy misalignment below are common. These ideas can serve as points to review within your own organization. The objective with this chapter is help you have different conversations with your team. Ask questions to determine if there is understanding of the vision. Allow yourself to ask tougher questions to confirm alignment with the business objectives and what sales leadership is thinking, saying, and doing. However, the fastest way to understanding is an evaluation and improvement analysis of the sale organization. (See "Exclusive Reader Bonus Page").

Examples:

1. **Business Strategy:** Weak Integration of Company Vision with Coaching

2. **Marketing Strategy:** Marketing Tactics Not Supported by Sales Competencies

3. **Sales Strategy:** Increase Account Revenue and Maintain Margin Integrity

<u>Weak Integration of Company Vision with Coaching</u>.

Business strategies are the backbone for revenue growth and a company trying to scale. haring the vision of the company with sales leaders and sales managers will support alignment. However, the vision and the "why" behind the vision must be consistently communicated with the sales reps by sales leadership in formal coaching, goal setting activities, and informal coaching opportunities. Sales managers have a responsibility to "connect the dots" between the business objectives and the salespeople's daily activity.

Sales managers should spend 50% of their time coaching salespeople on various issues. One aspect of coaching is sharing the "why" behind the metrics and tactics the salespeople are expected to meet. Consistent coaching from management on the strategic goals supports individual personal goal achievement. Coaching is impactful when the company vision is tied to the personal goals of the salespeople. This is how true alignment of all objectives are achieved.

Marketing Tactics Not Supported by Sales Competencies.

A marketing strategy might be attendance of trade shows and conferences. Significant resources are invested in attending trade shows and conferences—trade show booths, fees, staffing, and travel. This marketing strategy requires reps who are good at following up on leads (farmers), and great at qualifying leads at and during trade show follow-up.

Marketing effort should be aligned and support the sales strategy. The sales organization must have the skills to be effective at the tactics necessary to attain an ROI on the marketing spend.

Increase Account Revenue and Maintain Margin Integrity.

When the sales strategy is to increase volume with existing accounts, the pricing strategy must be aligned as well as considerations about product mix and share of wallet.

A failing strategy would be to grow revenue by discounting product pricing. Sales leadership must be diligent communicating that revenue growth cannot be achieved by discounting prices. Perhaps the customer needs just-in-time delivery of products or easier terms; these are better alternatives for value to a customer than reducing margins by lowering prices.

A sales leader can guide a sales rep to expand the number of contacts within the company. This can be accomplished by farther reach in the company either by geographic location or divisions to sell more of the same products to new buyers who are willing to pay a premium for value. Another tactic when there are many products that the customer currently purchases from other vendors is that the salespeople can begin to sell additional products or services—gaining the share of wallet with the customer.

Aligning the strategy with the sales skills is also important. The strategy might be to grow certain accounts from $100,000 to $200,000 in a year. Maintaining premium pricing and growing what the customer buys will require salespeople to have competencies in selling value, consultative selling, and reaching decision makers who care about value. The reps cannot answer RFQs and sell to the procurement department. They must have the skills to call higher into the customer and find the reasons the customers will pay for value. If the sales competencies do not exist with the sales team, there isn't alignment with the strategy.

These examples are only a few areas where business, marketing, and sales strategies can go sideways. When considering your objectives, review the team's ability to execute. The vision does not need to change. However, expectations for the timeline may need to reset temporarily as the team is upskilled and augmented.

Questions for contemplation.

- Can our sales leadership articulate the vision for the company?

- Do the sales managers coach the salespeople enough, and consistently connect the personal goals with the company objectives?

- Does our pricing strategy support our business objectives?

- Does the sales team have the competencies and beliefs to execute on the sales strategy?

- Is the marketing strategy and spend aligning with the sales strategies?

Chapter 7

Critical Mistake #7

Making decisions without good data.

Does this scenario sound familiar? It is the end of the second quarter. The CEO is reviewing the sales reports and notices that the same four people are always the top four producers. After further analysis, the top two spots are always the same reps, with the same people being first and second. The third and fourth producers rotate their rankings, but are always third or fourth. The sales leader cannot definitively explain why Susan and Tony are always one and two. Vague answers about hard work and experience in the industry are offered by the sales leader.

The rest of the salespeople had similar patterns, with Jill and Hank missing their revenue objectives by 20% for the last six out of eight quarters. Upon further review, the CEO uncovers that the two quarters when Jill and Hank met their objectives, margins dropped from 35% to 25%. The top four producers' margins never dropped below 40%.

Again, the CEO asked the sales leader why this occurred and why it was tolerated. The sales leader offered platitudes like:

- *Some sales are just naturals, and know how to talk to customers.*

- *We cannot get rid of them because even at 75% to 80% of quota, we need the revenue.*

- *The motivational training we did last quarter did not resonate with everyone.*

- *When I got meetings with Jill and Hank, I always needed to step in to get the deal closed; they can only take it so far.*

The sales leader accepted that the sales team would always have a few Jill and Hank type reps, yet could not figure out how to help them or coach them out. Unfortunately, many CEOs accept this refrain. <u>This is the seventh critical mistake—not understanding the strengths and weaknesses</u>

<u>of the salespeople, sales managers, systems and processes, sales hiring processes, and sales leadership.</u>

I believe CEOs make great decisions when they have good data. Don't believe the myth that top salespeople are mysterious *Wizards* and *Sorcerers* who have magical qualities. This is crap!

Of course, there is an art to sales. There are nuances in an ability to create rapport quickly, and being conversational and empathetic, yet skeptical with prospects can be learned. The science of sales is what the sales leader and the CEO in our story are missing.

Understanding why the top salespeople are in sales is vital when there is an economic downturn or a recession. The CFO is demanding that costs be cut, and this must include sales. A CFO will typically look at overhead and revenue to determine who should go and who should stay. Seems logical, but when no one at the company understands why some salespeople are successful and others are not, the CFO's method is will lead to more significant problems.

In difficult economic times, prospects and customers respond very much like the CFO. They put pressure on reps for discounts. The average order size drops. Customers begin to entertain conversations with competitors, and some start to give some of their business to your competitor. A loss in market share requires salespeople to go hunt for new logos. These are real issues that happen repeatedly with each recession or inflationary time.

The CFO convinces the CEO to let 40% of the sales team go. The business strategy is to reduce overhead. The sales strategy is to go add new customers and take customers from the competitors. *The CFO is asking the sales team to do more with less.* The CFO understood that the large long-term customers revenue dropped about 15% during an economic downturn, so adding a few new customers would carry the day. The sales strategy was to become a predator and go win new business.

In this scenario, Jill and Hank are gone, as well as three other salespeople. Susan and Tony stay because they are consistently top producers. Some of the middle-of-the-road producers were let go. The CFO's decision criteria were average account size, payroll overhead, and compliance with policies the CFO deemed important.

Jill and Hank plus three mid-level producers were recommended for termination. Reps like Nick—who sold new companies, but his average orders were 11% lower than the top four reps, and who had earned a few bonus checks for creating new accounts—were let go. Nick also was not great about turning in expense reports on time.

If you recall, the sales leader could not identify why Susan and Tony were top producers. The assumption made by leadership is that shedding salespeople based on overhead and revenue, and reps like Susan and Tony can go hunt or gain new business.

The salespeople retained were consistent producers. The shallow evaluation of overhead and revenue left a significant gap in the team's ability to be successful. The salespeople left were not <u>hunters</u>. Tony and Susan were strong account managers. They managed large accounts that generated revenue. For example, Susan and Tony worked twenty accounts each that ebbed and flowed business. Some accounts were strong in Q1 and Q2, others were buyers in Q3 and Q4. They managed the accounts well by growing their contacts, working through politics in the organization, and followed up a lot.

Susan and Tony had NOT opened a new account in five years. It felt like they did because new divisions within the same company structure would start to order. The same procurement group supported all the divisions. Susan and Tony did a great job as strategic account managers, but they did not have the competencies to hunt new business consistently. If the CEO had this information, and the appropriate analysis was done, the salespeople who had opened up new accounts consistently, but didn't have any big accounts, might have been retained.

Susan and Tony would have been retained, but their focus would have on retention and protecting their accounts from competitors. Given the CFO's analysis, there was pressure on Account Managers to open new accounts and double down on retention. Without the hunting skills and the will to prospect consistently, the risk is higher to fail at both.

Releasing Jill and Hank was warranted, but the reps generating new logos should have been retained. Sales managers would need to be more diligent about coaching the salespeople, making sure pipelines were full, steps in the sales process weren't missed, and maintaining accountability to the modified metrics for prospecting.

This fictional story plays out consistently in the real world. Large, mid-size, and small companies all make these critical mistakes. However, there is a way to have all the data uncovered for the unique situation at your company.

The are twenty-one core sales competencies, twenty core required sales management competencies, and nine leadership qualities. To understand the sales organization from top to bottom is to understand the strengths and weaknesses of the people and the processes. The most accurate, objective, and efficient means to gather the insights required to make lasting change in a sales organization is understanding the sales force—understanding their Will to Sell, Sales DNA, and Sales Competencies.

There is a sample report in the resources for this book that illustrates all of the competencies. I would encourage you to review these competencies, and consider how the information would help improve sales performance.

www.waltercrosby.com/resources

There is a solution to gather the information a CEO needs to make great decisions. *The final section of this short book will provide you with a way to gather the missing insights.*

Questions for contemplation.

- Does the sales leader understand the strengths and weaknesses of the salespeople?

- Does the sales leader know what the right mix of account managers, farmers, and hunters are required to execute on the sales strategies in good times as well as recessionary periods?

- Does the sales organization have the right metrics for the various reps on the team?

- How can the sales leader effectively manage and coach the team without knowing their strengths and weaknesses?

- Can the sales team be more effective?

- How much more effective can they be?

PART III

The next three chapters provide context for you to work with your sales manager. I provide you with frameworks and questions to ask your manager. If you engage with them, you will begin to understand if you have the right person in the right seat.

Sales management is difficult. Sales managers don't know what they don't know. And, they default to behaviors that create wins in the short term, but destroy long term growth. You want your sales manager to make Heroes, not be one.

You want accountability. People write about it, and talk about it. I share an accountability framework that your sales manager can implement tomorrow. It is the same process we teach in our 90-day sales manager program. It is simple to use, and does not need technology.

Mechanics and Maintenance

The seven fundamental reasons for inaccurate revenue fore-casts are caused by neglect and oversight in the sales orga-nization. Just like with your vehicle, the basics of the car must be maintained for safe driving. Regular maintenance of things like the oil, brakes, tires, changing filters, spark plugs, windshield solvent, and fuel.

Your sales managers may not be a good mechanic or even know how many spark plugs your engine has. This chapter will provide you the framework to ensure the sales engine is properly maintained.

Let me share a secret about sales management. Great sales managers don't manage salespeople. Great sales managers set clear expectations around leading indicators, and a op-timized sales process. Sales management is process driven. Accountability to a sales process with clear expectations will elevate average salespeople to above average—and this will give you the ability to scale the team.

Next, you must hold your sales manager accountable to the steps describe herein. The sales manager must hold your salespeople accountable.

"By changing nothing, nothing changes."
—Tony Robbins

You may as well stop reading, if you are not willing to create accountability.

I will give you the framework for you to work with a sales manager, and the sales manager's workbook will give the sales manager a framework to hold salespeople accountable. The important point is the accountability principles I describe are simple to understand, and implementation are critical to improvement.

There are 3 possible solutions to create accountability:

1. You decide this is important enough to solve, and you invest the time to coach your sales manager to better performance, and fix the revenue forecast; 60-90 minutes a week.

2. Assign the accountability of the sales manager and the follow up to someone on your leadership team, i.e. a CFO or Finance is usually good with accountability. They must establish a professional relationship with the sales management; nor should you abdicate the entire process. You must check in with the everyone along the way.

3. Hire a professional coach for the sales manager to hold them accountable. The coach must have a plan and experience. Helix offers this service if you want to pay for speed.

Regardless of your choice, an accurate and reliable forecast requires everyone on the team to have clear expectations. The sales manager will need to make changes to how they manage the sales pipeline. They will have to change the expectations of the salespeople, and you must reset the expectations of the sales managers. Everyone will need clear guidelines and standards for what is required!

Here's why... You already have the evidence of what weak processes and ineffective accountability deliver. A crappy revenue forecast! Let's fix the problems once and for all.

The following chapters provides the path to solve the problem of an unreliable revenue forecast using a step-by-step process. I am going to share a few resources along the way that will support your progress.

Your situation is unique, so read through the description of each problem, and the solution. You will need to assess how much of a problem the particular step is at your company. Rest assured; each is a problem to some degree. The only question is to what level.

Hero vs. Hero Maker

Sales managers can be a huge asset to a company, if trained to coach and hold salespeople accountable. They must spend most of their time coaching salespeople; most means 50% to 60% of their time.

A common mistake sales managers make is taking the role of HERO. It looks or sounds like this: instead of taking the time to coach and train a rep when an issue arises, the sales manager jumps into the fray, leaving the rep on the outside looking in, the manager does the work, and closes the sale. Hero in action.

The rep learns nothing, and needs the sales manager the next time for when the same situation happens. This is not scalable. The sales manager wimps out instead of doing the work that will support the long-term growth of your rep.

This hero behavior has a negative effect on your sales culture, and the growth of the team. Some reps will not bring learning opportunities to the sales manager because they feel they will be taken out of their own deals and diminished!

Another common problem with sales managers is they are not prepared for the role. Too often, a sales manager gets promoted because they were a great salesperson. The skill sets required for great sales management are different—following a process, being patient and helping the reps, being a great communicator of expectations, and strong enough to hold the reps accountable to your process.

Someone needs to support and coach the sales manager. Large companies have a VP of Sales. Smaller companies the sales manager who is left on an island. If you don't have both roles, you will need to be the sales leader, or hire a <u>fractional sales leader</u>. A fractional service provider allows you to leverage years of experience without the hit to payroll.

The sales leader or the acting sales leader must be coaching the manager on:

- Running sales meetings that refresh sales skills and share best practices.

- Debriefing reps after a sales meeting or call.

- Provide pre-call planning,

- Train the team on the sales process & methodology.

- Holding monthly accountability meetings.

- Monthly Pipeline Reviews.

- Coach sales techniques.

We have a *sales management playbook* that can help you and your team get better at each of the above. Because you have this book, you have a free 90-day subscription to our **Helix Sales Academy**. We update resources, and training materials regularly.

The Helix Sales Academy gives you and your team the fundamentals that are usually missing. Sales managers cannot be responsible for something they don't understand, and training on fundamentals is rare. And most CEOs believe that their Sales Manager is prepared for their role. Sadly, they are not.

Let me explain sales managers who are coachable will embrace the opportunity to learn. Some may struggle, but give them a fighting chance. Those who push back may not be open to coaching or the direction you need to take the sales organization. Regardless, you must hold them accountable or move on.

The accountability framework is a set of questions you can ask your sales manager. You will immediately know if the sales manager gets it or if they need support and coaching.

Here are 6 coaching questions you can ask your sales manager along the way. *By the way, they work with all your managers.*

> 1. What is your approach to make the change?
>
> 2. What resources will you use or need?
>
> 3. How will you introduce this to the team?
>
> 4. What is your plan to train & coach the team?
>
> 5. What is your accountability plan for the team?
>
> 6. What is your continuous improvement plan?

The accountability comes with the follow up on each step. The sales manager must show you the agreed upon outcome.

All six cannot be implemented at once. The accountability partner must collaborate and support the sales managers growth. A time frame is set for each step.

Accountability is critical for success!

It is common for the CEO to get busy, and let accountability slide. It happens a lot! Failure is inevitable without accountability. Your revenue forecast will be wrong, and the effort will be for naught.

KEY LEARNING TAKE-AWAYS

- Sales managers are often not prepared for the job. They need help. If you do not have a VP of Sales, you must coach the sales manager on these elements or find a strong manager in your organization to support the sales manager.

- There are fractional providers and outsourced resources, but we recommend engaging with the sales manager using these ideas. You will gain insights into their competencies. We offer an evaluation of sales managers.

- Share our Free resources in the **Helix Sales Academy** with the sales manager. The sales management resources provide instruction to implement the fundamentals of sales management. If they engage with these resources, it is a good indication the manager is coachable.

CEO'S AUXILLARY QUESTIONS TO SALES MANAGER:

- How much time do you spend on coaching the team each week?

- How much time do you spend understanding the metrics and tracking if sales performance is improving?

- Do you know what motivates each salesperson?

- How do you think all of this affects the revenue forecast?

An Accountability Framework

A high performing sales culture requires accountability. It is important for business owners to understand; to attract and retain elite salespeople you cannot accept mediocrity from the team. Top sales talent holds themselves accountable and do not want to associate with poor performers.

If you believe holding people accountable is a negative attribute, and contradicts your company culture, sorry, but you are wrong. I advocate for a carrot not the stick.

High achieving sales people love accountability because they achieve results. When they miss, they know it. Great salespeople want constructive feedback. Weak salespeople don't like accountability or coaching because it makes them uncomfortable.

Accepting mediocrity in a sales organization is a slippery slope that requires significant work to change. If your sales culture has allowed mediocrity to become normal, this must change.

A tip to accountability for salespeople is to tie personal goals of sales reps to the goals of the company. Everyone wins. Hold a goals workshop and connect what salespeople want personally to a sales objective. This is leverage. What do they want to buy? A boat, house, college tuition for their kid... something big that takes time. The leverage comes from the conversation— "How are you going to get the new house if you don't make the outbound calls?"

If accountability is a bad word in your sales organization, you probably have weak salespeople, and/or weak sales management. You can begin to change this by supporting the sales manager. It will take time, but you can build momentum.

Here is a 15-minute accountability meeting structure that is effective, avoids micromanagement, and shines a light on the poor performers. It will help weed out the non-performers.

TIMING.

- The accountability meeting is scheduled immediately after the first of month; as soon as the sales manager has the previous month's revenue figures.

- The meeting is scheduled, and on the calendar. It is not hallway conversation.

- The meeting is scheduled for 15 to 30-minutes.

FRAMEWORK.

1. Revenue is reviewed. Was the goal achieved or not? If the monthly revenue objective was achieved, the manager should celebrate this with the rep. If achievement is consistent (three months in a row), the rep is being accountable to the goals.

2. If revenue objectives are not consistent, the pipeline is reviewed for health, size, what is new, and what has been advanced since the last meeting.

3. Did the sales activities, prospecting, meetings meet the KPIs agreed to?

DELIVERY.

1. If the revenue is achieved, the meeting is over. Accountability achieved. If achieving revenue goals is uncommon with the rep, a look at the pipeline to ensure it is robust and healthy is a prudent practice. This can be achieve in a few minutes.

2. If the revenue goal is missed, the sales manager must look at the health of the rep's sales pipeline for size. Size is determined by the annual revenue goal divided by the rep's win rate percentage. Sales manager must also ask what was added and advanced in the process since the last meeting. If the pipeline is healthy, the meeting may end. 10 minutes.

3. If the revenue goal is missed, and the pipeline is weak, the sales manager has no recourse but to look at KPIs. Is the rep doing enough prospecting? It is not micromanagement because the rep failed to meet the objectives. The rep must be held accountable to the expectations if they are not doing the work. A few months in a row of this, the rep either is performing, or you know they must be replaced.

KEY LEARNING TAKE-AWAYS.

- The 15-minute accountability meeting is easy and effective.

- Accountability must be consistent. Creating accountability with salespeople is as easy as following a simple process that is effective, and efficient.

- Sales managers must be fair, but tough. The expectations are referenced, and the manager must leverage the personal goals of the rep.

- High performing sales teams expect and accept responsibility for their actions.

ACCOUNTABILITY FRAMEWORK FOR SALES MANAGER.

1. Are you using the accountability framework?

2. Which step is causing you challenges?

3. Are you being consistent with scheduled accountability meetings?

4. What is your plan to coach the team?

5. What exactly are the expectations you have set for each rep?

6. What support do you need to implement a consistent accountability plan?

7. What is your continuous improvement plan?

CEO'S AUXILLARY QUESTIONS TO SALES MANAGER:

- What are the metrics in place to measure success monthly?

- What is your approach to establishing accountability with the team? Frequency?

- Are you using the technology to make these accountability meetings efficient for everyone?

- How do you think all of this affects the revenue forecast?

PART IV

I Don't believe in Sales Training... Early

This chapter will upset sales consultants. Sales training is a waste of time and resources unless the training is supported by the sales organization to change habits and mindsets. In order to become proficient at a skill, time and effort is required. This does not happen in a training workshop, a seminar, or without the infrastructure in the sales organization. Let's not waste resources.

Athletes and salespeople are often compared to each other. However, there is little in common between professional athletes and salespeople. There is less in common between a sports organization and a business.

Sports teams are organized to compete, and some are designed to win. Business of all sizes struggle to compete because they lack the structure. I believe the culture, sales, systems, processes, and management of the sales organization (the fundamentals) drive competition and a winning attitude on the sales team.

It starts early.

It is relatively easy for a kid to get on any type of team as an eight-year-old. Baseball, dance, soccer—the bar is very low. Show up, sign a release, get mom to pay a fee, and poof—the kid is an athlete with a uniform and everything.

The barriers to get an entry level sales position are equally modest. Young athletes and newly minted salespeople can learn the rules of the game on the job and are taught some fundamentals (poorly). They are on the path to the big leagues!

Athletics and sales begin to diverge immediately. Even at a young age, athletes practice. It does not matter if it is a team sport or an individual sport like golf or tennis, athletes practice. The organizations that manage and operate the sports teams demand practice and improvement to progress to higher levels of competition. They require standards just to make the cut and earn a spot on a team.

Consider your sales organization.

- Is your sales leader running two-a-day practices to get the team in shape? Of course not.

- Are they spending time at sales meetings working on sales skills (not product knowledge)?

- Do they practice how to begin a prospecting call?

- Do they work on developing killer questions to ask prospects in discovery meetings?

- Are managers modeling the right behaviors for outbound activity?

- Does sales leadership make sure the reps are taking the buyer through the same process consistently?

If the answers are no, it is not entirely their fault. No one showed them how to do it during their career. And you or whoever hired the sales manager assumed they knew what to do. Perhaps hoped they knew? Hope is not a quality strategy.

Who is coaching?

The athlete and salesperson metaphor breaks down again with coaching. Athletes seek out coaching. Top athletes like Michael Jordan, Kobe Bryant, and Charles Barkley paid for additional training and coaching to give themselves an edge. Salespeople are not inclined to practice because it is uncomfortable and not the policy in most sales organizations.

Role-playing conversations in a conference room with salespeople is a safe and effective way for a salesperson to quickly gain feedback and improvement for their conversations with prospects. Recording prospecting calls and a sales manager coaching an actual call is another form of practice that is shunned by salespeople and sales managers. Not because it doesn't work, but because few leaders require it, encourage it, model it, or know how to do it.

Sales training can work. However, it takes what I call the fundamentals:

- A culture of accountability and high-performance standards

- A coaching mindset by sales managers and sales leaders

- Practice until the individual owns it

- The time to develop the new habits required to be effective

- A sales process that fits with the methodology taught in the training

When the fundamentals are in place, sales training will work because it is supported. When you have the fundamentals in the sales organization, identifying, hiring, and onboarding new salespeople is much easier. The model for the candidate exists, and the infrastructure is known by all.

Typically, the last thing I do with clients is a training program. The training will not be sticky if the fundamentals are not there. The training will not be effective if the salespeople do not see a path to reaching their goals by participating. Sales training will not work unless sales managers understand and coach the team. In sports parlance, if the fundamentals are not practiced and practiced well, how can someone be in the right position to hit the ball, make the tackle, take the shot, or close the deal?

If it was easy for salespeople to excel, they would simply take a seminar or read a book and become a superstar. t obviously does not work that way. The good news is that it does not take a lifetime for a salesperson to become good. It does take the fundamentals and your commitment to winning.

This all may seem daunting. That's okay. Take a breath and finish the book. There are resources to guide you to a good solution for your team and your company, and to help you realize your dream.

How I Help Visionary CEOs and Entrepreneurs?

Since you reached this far in the text, there is a good chance that at least one of the critical issues described resonated with you. The approach I take to solving the challenges in a sales organization is simple and straightforward. You may find the solutions appropriate, but you are not sure how to start.

My approach is to be all-in solving sales problems. I create lasting relationships with CEOs, sales managers, and salespeople. However, I may not be the guy to help you and your sales team. The criteria for me to work with a CEO is that we share five attributes that drive success:

1. **Data driven analysis**.

2. **Principled strategies.**

3. **Unique Battle Plan**.

4. **Measurable Results**.

5. **GRIT.** *The commitment and the desire to win.*

The best way to describe how I help a visionary CEO is to imagine the journey to your vision. We walk the path together. Traveling shoulder to shoulder. We see the same landscape and have the same view of what lies ahead. However, our perspectives are unique. Each through the lens of our own experience and expertise. The process is collaborative, yet guided. The path will be challenging at times, but the destination is always rewarding.

The people I help will have one or more of these monikers: Entrepreneur, CEO, President, Visionary, and Integrator. They lead a company under $75M, but trying to reach the next significant revenue milestone feels just beyond their grasp. Scaling. Growing Revenue. A reliable revenue forecast. A sales organization that befuddles them or has gotten away from them.

The company is always B2B with a complex sale, and usually has a top-quality product or service with premium pricing.

Though the company's products and services vary, these five are consistent themes among my clients:

- They sell products that they manufacture

- They distribute products direct to end users

- The company is a professional service provider or creative agency.

- They manage IT services and software

- The company sells product into the commercial construction process, often commoditized.

The common thread of those that I help is a hidden obstacle existing within the sales organization. For the CEO, the situation is frustrating because they cannot identify the underlying problems.

Individually, the seven problems I described earlier in this book can cause a variety of challenges that are not easily tied back to the root cause. However, when there is a combination of the obstructions occurring at the same time, the situation moves from frustration to one that requires deep analysis and understanding.

Sure, if time is not an issue, tinkering with the sales organization will eventually work. How much time is necessary?

The only approach I know that creates consistent results is to rip off the Band-Aid and understand the sales organization's strengths and weaknesses. Once a visionary leader understands what was hidden from them with solid recommendations, that leader always sees the way forward.

I believe the CEO, when presented the facts, makes good decisions. The way I help is to present the facts and findings that shine a light on the underlying obstacles. I recommend which problem to remove first because it makes the next obstruction easier to eliminate. The only thing left to do is to get to work helping the CEO grow revenue.

The Next Step

So, what do you do now? You have options.

<u>Option 1</u>.
Do nothing. *Transformation is difficult.*

<u>Option 2.</u>
Do it yourself. You lead the charge! This is viable if you have the GRIT and a team that you can motivate. Use the resource page for support. Happy to chat if you want.

<u>Option 3.</u>
This is the most difficult. Make a decision that change is a must. Decide that the changes to sales fundamentals will help you realize your vision faster.

If and when you make that decision, ask yourself these three questions and ponder the answers.

1. Did any of the seven critical mistakes described in this book feel like a problem you have? In other words, do you think I understand some of the challenges that are occurring at your company?

2. Do you think my experience, style, and approach has merit and is a fit for your style and experience?

3. Would you like some help?

If you answered yes to all three of those questions, we should talk.

The next step is to schedule a 90-Minute Consultation. No pitch. The cost of the consultation is our time and a <u>decision</u>. These three decisions are perfectly acceptable at the end of a 90-minute conversation.

1. A decision to do nothing. We both probably learned something.

2. Decide to have another conversation. Most common.

3. Decide to move forward. This happens only when the CEO has pressure to change.

Meet Walter Crosby

HE IS ON A MISSION TO HELP CEOs AND EN-TREPRENEUERS REALIZE THEIR VISION BY CRE-ATIUNG HIGH-PERFORMANCE SALES ORGANI-ZATIONS.

As CEO of Helix Sales Development, Walter engages with growth-minded CEOs who have the desire and commitment to build a performance-based sales culture. His clients say the journey can be challenging; however, the results are transformative—repeatable revenue growth with margin integrity.

He holds an advanced degree from the school of hard-won wisdom, as well as the University of Michigan. Frustrated by the lack of training every time he was promoted to management roles, he started his own firm to coach, train, and support successful sales teams.

His rocket fuel comes from coaching committed sales professionals to excel beyond what they thought was possible.

Those who know him best often find him reflecting over a fine cigar in his private cigar lounge. In fact, you can hear Walter share his thoughts weekly on his podcast, *Sales and Cigars*.

Sales and Cigars Podcast

Sales and Cigars is about two of my passions—sales and cigars. The podcast is not a scripted *ask the guest to answer the same five questions each week*. I engage with business owners, CEOs, sales leaders, salespeople, and sales managers about sales. How they think about sales and what to do to gain an advantage in the market.

My guests and I talk about real life struggles and solutions. We cover best practices and share ideas. The objective is to have interesting conversations about sales and business that are fun for me and educational for the listener.

Sales and Cigars is not Gladys and Myrtle sitting at the kitchen table talking about quilting. No offense, Gladys. We dig into the reasons salespeople suck, and what they need to do to get better. I have a monthly series with my colleague,

Nate Tutas, called *How to think about Sales*. Nate and I geek out about the details and the fundamentals.

You can find *Sales and Cigars* on Apple and Spotify. You can subscribe at

www.SalesandCigars.com

Go grab a cocktail, a cigar and strap in for a great conversation!

Exclusive Reader Bonus Page

The resource page at www.waltercrosby.com/resources is a special gift to my readers. It has access to information that CEOs can use to make changes to their sales organization, but also help understand what is happening under the surface. I update this page on a regular basis.

I am also making a private offer for readers. You can schedule a 90-minute consultation with me to discuss your situation and help you make progress. The objective of the consultation is to help you.

I typically call this an audit of the sales organization. It is a tight 90-minutes to discuss any combination of six elements listed below. You pick.

- Sales Culture

- Sales Structure

- Salespeople

- Sales Management

- Sales Leadership

- Sales Hiring

There is no time for a pitch during this consultation, so it is NOT a pitch. We dive into your specific situation and your needs.

The usual fee for the Sales Audit is $1,500. If you schedule the time through the unique link at the bottom of the page, or to me directly and mention this page, the fee is waived.

We will ask each other a lot of questions. My goal is to help. Maybe we work together, maybe not.

calendly.com/walter-helix/90-consultation-7-mistakes or just reach out to me and mention the book.

Access Reader Resources Here:

www.waltercrosby.com/resources